Wood Pallet Projects
23 Creative Ways To Reuse Old Wooden Pallets

Table of content

duction	3
Chapter 1	6
Chapter 2	11
Chapter 3	14
Chapter 4	16
Chapter 5	21
Conclusion	24

oduction

It is becoming increasingly popular to reuse everyday materials that we could just throw away. Many different communities of DIYers have expressed their skill reusing commonly discarded materials. Unlike recycling or dumpster diving however, reutilizing wooden pallets for your home is a creative endeavor and calls upon the crafters artisanship. Every design you see in this book can be finished and/ or painted after sanding granting it a custom look to seamlessly add to your home.

Pallets are often given away for free. To see if a business is willing to give away pallets, simply ask a teller or store manager. Taking pallets without permission of the establishment which used them can be regarded as stealing and is a crime. Make sure you begin every project the right way and ask before taking materials.

Not all pallets are created equal. There are square pallets, double sided pallets, painted/ treated pallets and rough pallets. For this book we will be assuming the pallet dimensions displayed on the left. This is a rectangular pallet with an average of 1 x 6 boards making up its surface, two long supports and three short supports. These pallets can have boards on both faces or just one, two way entry or four way entry. They may also have a varying degree of usable 1 x 6 bards.

This book will also require a variety of tools and hardware including: nails, screws, gloves, hammer, saw, crowbar, sandpaper, planer, paint and primer. Specific projects will call for: "L" brackets, eyelets, drywall screws, rope, screw in hooks, and carpet.

Before beginning any work with pallets, including transport, be sure to use thick gloves. Put on work goggles to protect your eyes from debris before using a planer, sandpaper, crowbar or saw.

Pallet Safety: While it is a great and easy idea to reuse and repurpose wooden pallets, there are a few key safety precautions to take before beginning any project.

Firstly, avoid any damaged pallets. If the pallet has a stain, it may be more than aesthetically displeasing, it could be dangerous. Toxic chemicals or bacteria may be on a wooden pallet so be sure you know where it came from. Avoid using wooden pallets with visual blemishes as they could be a sign of contamination.

The second thing to look out for his treated pallets. Most often labeled with a stamp, pallets which have been treated are often hazardous to one's health. There are many different stamps which might grace that perfect pallet. The one to look out for is the IPPC stamp/ logo. This will identify the pallet you have selected as being regulated by a organization with an interest in labeling harmful products. On the logo there may be following identifiers which are indicative of their hazard. Marks to look out for are: Regular scoring of the wood indicating pesticides. There may be sets of letters on the pallet which indicate if the wood has been treated or not. **[HT]** = is the abbreviation placed on labels used for pallets which have been Heat Treated. **"MB"** being the letter pairing for wood treated with Methyl Bromide.

Checking all pallets to ensure they are safe for use will increase the viability, aesthetic and longevity for your creative project. Don't put yourself, your animals, or your guests at risk because you forgot to check. KEEP IT SAFE.

For the sake of this book there will be 4 different **standards** to prepare your pallets.

1. Sand down all faces of the pallet. This will prevent splintering and give your project a cleaner look.
2. Sand down all faces of the pallet. Then, using a crowbar, carefully pry the planks of wood off of the upward facing side. Pallets may be reversible so keep the side which looks the best and remove the side with more damaged planks. If necessary, plane the wood before sanding.
3. Sand down all faces of the pallet. Then, using a crowbar, carefully pry the planks of wood off of the upward facing side. If necessary, plane the wood before sanding. Next, remove any nails which may have pulled through the planks from the major supports. Once the supports are fully exposed and nail free, begin prying the supports from the downward facing planks. Your bodyweight should be enough to leverage the supports free. If necessary, utilize a hammer or nail remover.
4. Completely disassemble pallet. Remove any nails and sand all pieces.

5. The more time you take to find undamaged pallets and to refine them to the "preparation standards" outlined above the better your final project will turn out.

Chapter 1

Yard

The garden is an excellent place to practice you pallet crafting skills. Especially if you are new to wood working. Because these constructions will be outside, they will not last as long as other projects without proper sanding and staining. For maximum results, treat wood with safe chemicals to protect against weather damage.

Please be sure to read the Pallet Preparation Standards which were outlined in the Introduction.

There are many different and artistic ways to reuse a wooden pallet as a garden box. Here are 3 easy styles to get you started. All 3 designs require builders to prepare their wooden pallets to the standard 1 described in the introduction.

Garden Box 1

This garden box is the most simple project in the entire book. It is to help crafters get familiar with the process of preparing the pallets and reutilizing planks which have been removed.

Step 1: Prepare one wooden pallet.

Step 2: Remove three or four of the upward facing 1x6 planks.

Step 3: Place Garden Box in location where planter is desired.

Step 4: Use the planks removed to cap the flat at either end. This will prevent soil from wearing out the sides.

Step 5: Fill with soil, plant seeds, and enjoy your garden box.

Garden Box 2

This garden box is a bit more complex. It will be possible to hang this planter upright on a wall given proper fastening.

Step 1: Take pallet, which has been prepared to standard 1 as outlined in the introduction, and pry every other upward facing 1 x 6 plank away from pallet.

Step 2: Measure distance between the two long supports.

Step 3: Cut 1x6 pieces which have been removed to fit between the long supports.

Step 4: Line up the cut pieces to be perpendicular to the remaining upward facing 1x6 boards. The pieces should slide snuggly between the long supports creating small troughs. Nail cut pieces to pallet.

Step 5. Rest pallet against wall with long supports vertical.

Garden Box 3

This is an ecofriendly way to reuse an old wooden pallet to make a vegetable garden.

Step 1: Prepare two pallets to standard 3 as outlined in the introduction.

Step 2: Remove short support leaving rectangle frame.

Step 3: Use 1 x 6 pieces to connect the two wooden frames.

Step 4: Place frames where they will be permanently resting.

Step 5. Remove ALL nails and hardware connecting frame and replace with wooden dowels. This will allow for the box to degrade into the soil over time.

Gardening Table

Build a place to set potted plants, tools and supplies. This two shelf table, if prepared properly, will serve your uses for years.

Step 1: Prepare two pallets to standard 2 and one pallet to standard 3.

Step 2: cut both pallets prepared to standard 2 in half.

Step 3: Nail long supports from the pallet prepared to standard 3 to two of the pallets cut in half. Repeat process for other two halves.

Step 4: Secure the two parts together to form a bench with two shelves.

Garbage Shed

Trying to keep critters from strewing trash all over your yard? Why not build a shed to enclose your trash barrels? It is a quick, easy and cheap way to keep pests and nosey paparazzi out of your trash.

Step 1: prepare eight pallets to level 2 standard and two pallets to the level 1 standard.

Step 2: Secure the two pallets prepared to standard 1 together on their short end. This will serve as your foundation.

Step 3: Set foundation where desired. It will become too heavy to move once walls are constructed.

Step 4: Using three pallets prepared to standard 2, secure them perpendicularly to the foundation. Two of the pallets should be lain horizontally with the third vertically.

Step 5: Using two more pallets prepared to standard 2, Build the long walls walls higher making sure to secure the walls to the vertical pallet for structural integrity.

Step 6: Using one pallet

Step ?: using pieces removed from pallets to prepare them for standard 2, build a door and fasten it to your structure with hinges. Note: the door may be too heavy for certain hinges so be sure to use load bearing hinges.

Compost Container

Looking for ways to reuse some of those splintered or extra pieces of lumber left over from previous projects? Reuse them in your eco-friendly compost container.

Step 1: Prepare nine wooden pallets to standard 1 as outlined in the introduction.

Step 2: Place one pallet on the ground in desired location.

Step 3: Securely nail a pallet to each side of the first pallet forming walls.

Step 4: Build up walls to desired height. If necessary, prepare another pallet to standard 4 and utilize its pieces to fortify the structure. Note: it is unnecessary and, in fact, unadvised to close up all of the gaps between 1 x 6 boards. Compost benefits from the permeation of wind and insects.

Step 5: Fill compost with scraps from other pallets. Do not include nails! And add a few shovels of dirt. Now you are ready to begin composting.

Chapter 2

For Pets

Pets are part of the family. Why not treat them with one of these creative pallet ideas? These designs are a bit more difficult than those outlined in Chapter 1. They will require a basic knowledge of carpentry and construction. For optimum results, it would be best use the instructions included in this chapter as a baser idea for pets house, tree or coup.

Dog house

Dogs need a place to hide from the rain or to beat the heat. Build them a home outside of home cheaply with the only limit being your own creativity. Some dogs may require larger homes. Increase design's pallet quantity accordingly to accommodate your animal.

Begin by preparing two pallets to standard 2, four pallets to standard 1, to standard 3 and two to standard 4.

Step 1: Place two pallets prepared to level 1 on the ground. These will serve as the base for your dog house. Secure them together using 1 x 6 boards gleaned from pallets prepared to standard 4.

Step 2: Cut supports gained from pallet prepared to standard 3 to equal length.

Step 3: Secure cut supports to the base pallets making a flat surface upon which to build the walls of your dog house.

Step 4: Secure three pallets, prepared to standard 1, on three sides of the foundation.

Step 5: On one of the longs sides, secure the fourth pallet (prepared to standard

Step 6: Using 1 x 6 boards, construct a roof making sure to leave no room for light or rain to permeate.

Step 7: With help from a friend, move doghouse to an area of your yard with as much natural protection from the elements as possible and watch your enjoy their new space.

Cat/ Ferret Tree

Cat trees are quick and easy to build. Most trees are covered in carpet so to complete this project you will need to pick some up from your local hardware store or look around for extra, free, materiel. Using the steps below as a guideline, make alterations to size or structure pattern to suit your cat or ferret.

Step 1: Prepare two Pallets to standard 4 and one pallet to standard 2 as outlined in the Introduction.

Step 2: Cut pallet prepared to standard 2 in half. Then cut one of those halves in half once more. Set two quarter pieces aside for the moment.

Step 3: Place half pallet on ground and use 1 x 6 boards from pallets prepared to standard 4 to frame half pallet. This will keep animals from climbing underneath your tree.

Step 4: Using 2 ¼ inch screws, secure long supports from pallet prepared to standard 4 together.

Step 5: Using 2 ¼ inch screws, secure two short supports from pallet prepared to standard 4 together.

Step 6: Fasten, using L brackets or 3 ½ in screws, two quarter pieces of pallet prepared to standard 2 perpendicularly to ends of columns made in steps 4 and 5. These will be the "islands."

Step 7: Secure column and islands to base.

Step 8: Using remaining pieces of pallet prepared to standard 4, make custom boxes, islands, shelves and ramps to best service your animal.

Step 9: Cover your cat tree in carpet to keep your animals paws safe.

Chicken coop

This is a quick and easy solution to a broken chicken coop. Though it is not ideal for long term use, a few modifications and personal know-how will maximize the longevity of this project.

Step 1: Take ten pallets which have been prepared to standard 1.

Step 2: Fasten 2 pallets together at their short end.

Step 3: place another pallet to be perpendicular to the pallets just put together. Repeat process around to form enclosed space.

Step 4: Add pallets, vertically, to increase height of the recently formed walls.

Step 5: Nail remaining two pallets together.

Step 6: Cap structure with the two pallets connected in step 5.

Step 7: Select an area for the entrance and cut. The pallet wood will cut from the structure in pieces so be careful.

Step 8: Screw hinges onto pieces cut from structure in step 7 and secure to the structure.

Chapter 3

Seasonal Items

One of the benefits to free material, outside of its unbeatable cost, is its relatively guiltless disposability. Once repurposed, even if worn out to their end, these designs will save you money and offer the opportunity to show of your seasonal style. The designs in this chapter vary in difficulty.

Temporary Pathway

Making a temporary pathway is perfect for homes often effected by tough-to-travers weather. Use this easy and clever idea to build walkways over snow or keep patio furniture out of the mud.

Step 1: Prepare two pallets the standard 1 as outlined in the introduction.

Step 2: Finish pallet to prevent weather damage.

Step 3: Fasten rope to corners of pallet. This will make them easier to move in the snow or mud.

Lawn Chair

Add a personal flare to any yard or deck with a pallet lawn chair. There are many different designs for chairs. Depending on what you are most comfortable in, design a chair that is right for you. As a result of the plethora of possibilities, this is one of the more technical designs described in this book and should only be attempted by those confident in their wood working skills.

Step 1: Prepare one pallet to standard 2 and two pallets to standard 4.

Step 2: Cut pallet prepared to standard 2 in half.

Step 3: Taking two long supports from pallet prepared to standard 4, fasten long supports together to form an "X" frame. The higher degree will define the degree of recline in the chair. Repeat this with the other set of long supports

Step 4: Cut ends of Long supports at the same degree as the shorter angler off the "X." This Angle must be exact for chair to rest evenly on the ground

Step 5: Connect two "X" frames, with one of the halves from Step 2, along the desired backrest angle. Note: You may substitute halves of pallet for 1 x 6 boards cut to desired length for the perfect width.

Step 6: Using 1 x 6 boards from pallet prepared to standard 4, connect the "X" frames to form the seat.

Step 7: Use remaining pieces to add arm rest.

Step 8: Sand all corners and edges of chair and stain.

Chapter 4

Custom Furnishing

Varying in difficulty, the designs outlined in this chapter will get you started on the bold goal of refurnishing your home in custom furniture. Perfect for people of all ages, satisfy your artistic ambitions through some of these spectacular home improvement ideas.

T.V. Rack

Buying a wall mount for your flat screen may be expensive.

Step 1: Prepare one pallet to standard 1

Step 2: Finish pallet to desired color and texture.

Step 3: Using your T.V as a guide, discover which of the boards should be removed for easier access to external inputs and outputs. Also take measurements and mark the pallet where you will attach hardware for T.V.

Step 4: Using proper hardware (i.e. nails, drywall screws) secure pallet to wall.

Step 5: Secure T.V.'s hardware to wall mount.

Shelf

One could always use more shelf space.

Step 1: prepare a single pallet to standard 4

Step 2: Cut one of the long supports into equal thirds. These will be your bracers.

Step 3: Secure bracers to wall at shelf's desired height. You may need to drill a pilot hole and/ or use drywall screws.

Step 4: Cut another support, this time with the product of three eight inch pieces.

Step 5: secure eight inch pieces to bracers.

Step 6: connect three bracers with 1 x 6 boards.

Shoe stand

Great for kids, this is a quick and cheap way to add a custom touch to any room.

Step 1: Prepare pallet to standard 1 in the introduction.

Step 2: Further sand the inside edges of the pallet then paint.

Step 3: After dry, lean pallet against a wall and use. If necessary, secure to wall using "L" bracket and drywall screws.

Pot Hanger

Many times new apartments do not have adequate space to store appliances and cookware in the kitchen. Instantly make a space for your pots and pans.

Step 1: Prepare pallet to standard level 2 as outlined in the introduction

Step 2: Secure Eyelets to wall eighteen inches higher than you would like the shelf to rest.

Step 3.Secure L brackets to wall at height you would like rack to sit.

Step 4: Drill pilot holes for screw in hooks.

Step 5: Screw hooks into flat.

Step 6: Secure load bearing chain or ropes to eyelets and to top of Pallet.

Step 7: Secure Pallet to L brackets.

T.V. Stand

Whether you've just moved in or are just redecorating a pallet made T.V. stand could be exactly what you need.

Step 1: Prepare one pallet to standard 1 and two pallets to standard 4.

Step 2: Cut pallet prepared to standard 1 in half lengthwise. Removing middle support may make this easier.

Step 3: Use to long supports from pallet prepared to standard 4 to along freshly cut edges. This would rebuild the frame on either piece to create two narrower pallets.

Step 4: Cut remaining long supports to equal length and short supports to same length.

Step 5: Connect rectangular frames made in step 3 with equal sized supports at their corners.

Step 6: Using 1 x 6 boards, increase structural integrity of your T.V. stand by hammering boards between long supports and pallet frames.

Coffee Table

Sometimes a DIY home needs a DIY coffee table. Add as much effort and creative ingenuity as possible while undertaking this simple project. Note: if you have made the T.V. stand or garden table the concept is relatively the same.

Step 1: Prepare two pallets to standard 1 and two pallets to standard 4.

Step 2: remove 1 x 6 boards from both pallets prepared to standard one.

Step 3: Nail or screw best looking boards side by side on the pallet frames. Try to leave as little room as possible between the boards

Step 4: Cut supports from pallets prepared to standard 4 to equal length.

Step 5: Connect supports to one of the rectangular frames made in step 3 with roughly 8 inches of support sticking out on one end.

Step 6: Standing the frame with supports upright, place the second frame on tope and secure to the supports. This will form the top surface of your coffee table.

Step 7: Sand top surface of table to make as even as possible then stain.

Bike Rack:

Are there a lot of bikes in your front yard? Do you often find yourself competing for a place to lock up your bike? Well try this quick and easy DIY pallet bike rack.

Step 1: You will need 2 Pallets per bike rack. Each rack holds between 3 and 5 bikes.

Step 2: Begin by preparing both pallets to the level one standard outlined in the introduction. Remove every other upward facing support from both pallets, keeping the first. Use pallets which line up and appear identical.

Step 3: Once prepared, take one long support from one of the pallets.

Step 4: Next, nail the support you just removed to the other pallet. The support should run along the pallet such that it is flush with the upward facing side keeping an even 90 degree angle.

Step 5: Now, nail the first flat to the second creating 90 degree "L" shape. Line up the gaps created in step 1. These gaps will host your bike tires.

Once firmly together, your bike rack is ready for use.

T.V. Tray

This is one of the most simple designs in this collection. Its simplicity simply leaves it open to quick customization.

Step 1: Prepare pallet to standard 4.

Step 2: Cut one of the long supports in half

Step 3: cut 3 1x6 boards in half.

Step 4: secure boards to supports.

Chapter 5

Custom Elegance

Just because you are using free materials doesn't mean your projects can't have an elegant feel. What you make and the time spent preparing the pallets can transform someone else's garbage into your custom home décor.

Book shelf

Great for kids, students and adults of all ages this book shelf will grant the element of artistic sophistication to anyone's book collection.

Step 1: Prepare a pallet to standard level 2 as outlined in the introduction.

Step 2: Cut the 1 x 6 pieces removed during the preparation to fit snuggly between the horizontal supports.

Step 3: Wedge cut pieces between supports long supports such that they rest on the short supports.

Step 4: Nail cut pieces perpendicular to short supports.

Step 5: Stand vertically against wall and secure with drywall screws.

Wine Rack

Everyone has a wine phase. Indulge in yours by making a custom wine rack for your home. It's a simple design that is easy to modify to fit your space's style.

Step 1: Prepare a pallet to standard 2 outlined in the introduction.

Step 2: Remove any boards that seem lose and replace them and the nails which secured them.

Step 3: Cut circles into 1x6 boards. Make varying sizes to support different bottle shapes.

Step 4: Sand edges of freshly cut holes.

Step 5: Using long supports from another project, build supports on the back side of the rack to keep it upright. This will also serve to keep your wine bottles from slide down behind the rack.

Step 6: Stain and finish wood.

Tool Mount

Get your garage organized with this quick and easy tool mount. Display your tool on a custom rack you made with them.

Step 1: Prepare pallet to standard 2 as described in the introduction.

Step 2: Place pallet face down with the exposed supports facing upward.

Step 3: Install wall mounts. Then install mounts, where desire, on the wall.

Step 4: Flip pallet over with supports facing down and 1x6 boards accessible.

Step 5: Place tools which will be mounted on pallet. Use pencil or chalk to outline where tools will hang.

Step 6: Drill pilot holes for hooks. Then, carefully hand screw in tool hooks.

Head Board

The headboard is a very simple yet elegant project that should be done when one is feeling confident in their wood working abilities. A very strait forward project with varying methods of completion, building a headboard is a job for the builder looking to stretch those artistic muscles.

There are no real steps to this project beyond breaking down a pallet, finishing the pieces with desired stain or paint and assembling. The key to a great DIY headboard is attention to detail. The supports will be the frame for your headboard. Otherwise the design is complete up to you. If you have done even a few of the other projects in this book, making a headboard from the lumber obtained from a couple pallets will be no problem.

Conclusion

All of the instructions included in this book are simple, easy and affordable ways to furnish your living space. Add a personalized element to your home in an age of Target and Ikea generic décor. Even if you aren't sure how you will use the pallets, it is always a good idea to keep an eye out for them. You never know when the creative bug will inflict you with the desire to build something unique and beautiful.

Making your own furniture and appliances out of reusable material is becoming more popular by the day. Those who are creative, eco-conscious or just crafty have pioneered this new and vibrant community of builders. There are hundreds of other schematics online with pictures, how-to-guides, forums and reference material. The possibilities are endless.

Consider the designs and instructions included in this book as a template for future designs. They are practice for the masterpiece you are yearning to make. There are so many ways to reuse wooden pallets. Expanding off of some of the ideas outlined in "DIY Wood Pallet Projects: 23 Creative Ways to Reuse Old Wooden Pallets for Decorating Your Space" will help make your custom home designs even more unique. Perhaps you have come up with a new project all your own reusing wooden pallets.Share your success stories along-side your horror stories in the ever growing community of artistic do-it-yourselfers

Remember, the more time you take to plane, sand and properly prepare your pallets the better the finished product will look. If you are conducting multiple projects, it is wise to save your left over pieces of lumber for future projects, firewood or compost. Reusing wooden pallets is eco-friendly and tax free, so don't hesitate to get absorbed in a new project part of the way into another. There are no downsides to making wooden pallet furniture or appliances.